Five-Minute Whodunits

Stan Smith

Illustrated by Lucy Corvino

Sterling Publishing Co., Inc.
New York

To three special Smiths:
my wife, Julie, and my parents, Peter and Lucile

"Crime is common. Logic is rare. Therefore it is upon the logic rather than upon the crime that you should dwell."

—*Sherlock Holmes*

Library of Congress Cataloging-in-Publication Data

Smith, Stan (Stanley E)
   Five-minute whodunits / Stan Smith ; illustrated by Lucy Corvino.
     p. cm.
   Includes index.
   ISBN 0-8069-9402-9
   1. Puzzles. 2. Detective and mystery stories. I. Title
GV1507.D4S55 1997
793.73—dc21   96-37009
                                               CIP

10 9 8 7 6

Published by Sterling Publishing Company, Inc.
387 Park Avenue South, New York, N.Y. 10016
© 1997 by Stanley Smith
Distributed in Canada by Sterling Publishing
^c/o Canadian Manda Group, One Atlantic Avenue, Suite 105
Toronto, Ontario, Canada M6K 3E7
Distributed in Great Britain and Europe by Cassell PLC
Wellington House, 125 Strand, London WC2R 0BB, England
Distributed in Australia by Capricorn Link (Australia) Pty Ltd.
P.O. Box 6651, Baulkham Hills, Business Centre, NSW 2153, Australia
Manufactured in the United States of America
All rights reserved

Sterling ISBN 0-8069-9402-9

Contents

Mr. Thomas P. Stanwick

§

E VEN THOSE UNACQUAINTED with Thomas P. Stanwick are often struck by his appearance. A lean and lanky young man, he stands six feet two inches tall. His long, thin face is complemented by a full head of brown hair and a droopy mustache. Though not husky in build, he is surprisingly strong and enjoys ruggedly good health.

His origins and early life are obscure. He is undeniably well educated, however, for he graduated with high honors from Dartmouth College as a philosophy major and studied logic and history at Cambridge University for a year or two afterwards. He now lives alone (with a pet Labrador) in a bungalow in the New England town of Baskerville, not far from the city of Royston. His house is filled with books, chess sets, maps, and charts. He earns a living as a freelance editor of textbooks on geometry and American history.

Personally, Stanwick is good-humored and amiable. His relaxed manner conceals the strength of his convictions and the intensity of his intellectual interests. He enjoys the company of his many friends, but cherishes his personal freedom and independence. The regular patterns of his life suit him well, and the pursuit of wealth, fame, or power holds no attraction for him.

His main interests are his intellectual pursuits. First and foremost, he is a logician, particularly skilled in traditional formal deduction. As an incessant student of its theoretical and practical aspects, he is fascinated by all sorts of mysteries and puzzles. Aside from pure logic, other interests of his include philosophy, chess, history, music, mathematics, literature, and etymology. An avid bibliophile, he owns hundreds of books on those topics.

Stanwick's personal tastes are simple. A casual dresser, he almost never wears a tie. His eating preferences are old-fashioned and include beef and potatoes. An ardent Anglophile, he has several British habits acquired during his many long stays in England. He prefers tea to coffee, for example, and smokes a pipe.

Besides seeing his friends, Stanwick's favorite pastimes are reading and chess. He is also fond of hiking in the New England hills. He takes long travel vacations in the summertime and often visits England. Sometimes he stays with the Earl of Stanwyck, a distant relative, at the earl's East Anglian estate or at his country estate in Scotland. He also enjoys visiting London and Cambridge, where he has many friends from his student days. Back home in Baskerville, he carries on an active correspondence.

He spends many of his evenings conversing with friends at the Royston Chess Club and elsewhere. When he has a hand in investigating and solving crimes, it is usually through his friendship with Inspector Matt Walker, a promising detective on the Royston police force who is about five years older than Stanwick. They play chess together at the chess club on Thursday evenings, and Stanwick occasionally drops by police headquarters.

Stanwick's interest in criminal cases is purely that of a logician. In that capacity, as Walker would be the first to admit, he is frequently very useful.

The Case of the
Wells Fargo Money
§

THE DARING THEFT OF half a million dollars from a Wells Fargo armored truck captured the imagination of the entire Royston area. As the *Royston Gazette* excitedly summarized it, the truck had just been loaded with cash from the First National Bank on the afternoon of June 4 when two or three men appeared, overpowered the guards, piled the money into a pickup truck, and disappeared—all in less than five minutes.

The investigation was placed in the hands of Inspector Matthew Walker. His skillful inquiries led the police to three men who often worked together and were suspected of several lesser robberies.

Some 10 miles from the city, in the little town of Baskerville, Thomas P. Stanwick, the amateur logician, pushed aside a postal chess analysis and admitted the inspector to his bungalow.

"I'm delighted to see you, Matt," said Stanwick as they seated themselves in the living room. "I hear you've been doing fine work on this Wells Fargo case."

"Thanks, Tom." Walker smiled wearily. "All the public attention has put a lot of pressure on us to solve it and, if possible, recover the money."

"I've also heard you have some suspects under surveillance."

"That's right. This is strictly confidential, of course." Walker leaned forward in his armchair. "We have conclusive evidence that Charles Acker, Bull Barrington, and Adam Crowley organized the job, and at least two of them actually carried it out. We've been monitoring their communications, hoping to get more information. The money has been hidden, and not all three of them know where it is. It would aid us enormously to find out who knows its location.

"To complicate matters, at least one of them communicates by a 'lying code', in which everything he says is false. The others speak truthfully. We don't know which, or how many of them, are using the lying code."

Stanwick idly twisted the tip of his mustache and chuckled.

"Quite a problem. Can I help?"

"I hope so." Walker flipped open his notebook. "These are the only helpful statements we've been able to intercept that might tell us who's lying and who knows where the money is:

> Acker: Barrington is using the lying code, and I know where the money is.
>
> Barrington : Acker was out of town at the time of the robbery.
>
> Crowley: Acker was in town at the time of the robbery if and only if he knows where the money is.
>
> Barrington: I don't use the lying code.
>
> Acker: Either I was in town at the time of the robbery or Crowley does not use the lying code.
>
> Crowley: Not all of us use the lying code. I don't know where the money is.

"As you can see, it's a bit of a tangle," Walker concluded.

Stanwick took and studied the notebook for a few minutes, and then handed it back.

"My dinner's almost ready," he said, standing up. "Pot roast, potatoes, and peas. Since you'll be working late anyway, I hope you can stay long enough to join me. In the meantime, I'll be glad to tell you who is lying, and at least one man who knows where the money is."

Who is lying? Who knows where the money is?

Solution on page 88.

A Slaying in the North End
§

"**W**ELL, MATT, WHAT big-city crimes are testing the skills and trying the patience of Royston's finest this week?"

Thomas P. Stanwick, the amateur logician, grinned at Inspector Walker as he dropped into the visitor's chair of the inspector's chronically cluttered office. Stretching his long legs toward the desk, he fumbled for his pipe.

Walker looked up wearily.

"Good to see you, Tom. I thought you were all tied up with that geometry textbook revision."

"That should be finished by Friday," replied Stanwick, lighting his briar. "By next Wednesday, I'll be off to London and Cambridge for two weeks of loitering, puttering in musty bookshops, and reminiscing about student days. What's up, though? You look frazzled."

"I sure am." Walker pawed through a pile of papers on his desk and pulled out four. "These are my notes on the Minot Street shooting. I've been up all night compiling them. There are still several gangs fighting up there in the North End. Les Chaven, the leader of the Blackhawks, was shot and killed last Friday afternoon by a member of the Leopards, apparently in a turf fight over Minot Street."

"So both gangs love Minot, eh?" said Stanwick.

Walker winced. "The members of the Leopard gang," the inspector continued, "are Al Foster, Bruce Diskin, Charlie Jensen, Damon O'Keefe, and Eddie Lyons. Their gang is pretty new, so we don't know yet which is the leader. Nor do we know which is the killer. So far, all I've been able to dig up are these facts:

"1. The killer and the leader had a fierce argument about whether to kill Chaven before deciding to go ahead with it.

"2. Jensen works the evening shift as a machinist in the local plant on weeknights and is thinking of working at his brother's gym-bag factory in San Francisco.

"3. The leader's wife is a teller at the Second National Bank. Foster, an only child, works part-time as a janitor there.

"4. The leader and Diskin play poker every Tuesday night at eight over Hiller's Saloon. Foster picks them up there after midnight and drives them home.

"5. Jensen is married to the killer's sister, who was once engaged to O'Keefe.

"6. O'Keefe, a bachelor, is the best lockpick of the five."

Stanwick, fingering the tip of his mustache, quietly glanced over Walker's notes and then handed them back. An amused twinkle lit his eye as he watched Walker give a gaping yawn.

"What you need," he said, "is a little more sleep. If you weren't so tired, I'm sure you'd see that there's easily enough information here to deduce the identities of both the leader and the killer."

Who is the leader? Who is the killer?

Solution on page 88.

Bad Day for Bernidi
§

DURING A MIDDAY VISIT to the city of Royston, Thomas P. Stanwick, the amateur logician, noticed several police cars at the entrance of Bernidi's, a small downtown jewelry store. Toying with the tip of his mustache in thoughtful curiosity, he approached and eased his way through a knot of onlookers. His friend Inspector Matt Walker was inside, and he signaled to the policeman at the door to let Stanwick in.

"Hello, Tom," exclaimed Walker in mild surprise. "What brings you here?"

"I was just passing by," replied Stanwick. He glanced around the cool, dark interior of the narrow room. "What happened?"

"I was just about to ask Mr. Bernidi to repeat his story to me."

The two turned to the small, white-haired owner, who was leaning against one of the two display counters that ran the length of both sides of the room. His face was streaked with dust, and he looked exhausted.

"I had just stepped into the back," he said, "when I hear the bell on the front door ring. I come out, and there's this guy, very well dressed, looking around and coming toward me and the register. 'Can I help you?' I say, and he smiles and pulls a gun halfway out of his jacket pocket. A little piece, but I can see it's real. Then he puts it back, but keeps his hand in there. There's nobody else around, so what can I do?

"Anyway, he makes me open the register, but I just made a deposit, so there's only a few bucks. He doesn't get mad, but takes a piece of clothesline out of another pocket, ties my hands behind my back, and makes me lie down on my stomach behind the side counter here, with my face to the wall.

"It was tight; you can see there's not much room back there. Then I hear him opening the wood panels—these here, the lower half of the counter—but he finds nothing. I only keep supplies down there. Then he steps across to the opposite counter, pulls out a little burlap sack, smashes the glass, scoops some rings into the sack, and runs out. I get up, see the broken glass, and yell for a cop."

"What did the man look like?" asked Walker.

"Like I told the officer—big, burly guy, clean-shaven, dark hair."

"Don't you have your display glass wired to an alarm?" inquired Stanwick.

"Never got around to it. It's insured, anyway."

"Well, thank you, Mr. Bernidi," said Walker, closing his notebook. "We'll check around and let you know when we make an arrest."

"I think you can make an arrest right now," said Stanwick quietly.

Whom does Stanwick suspect, and why?

Solution on page 88.

An Unaccountable Death

§

O**N THIS RAINY** T**UESDAY**, as on many other Tuesdays around
noon, Thomas P. Stanwick, the amateur logician, called on
his friend Inspector Matt Walker in the inspector's tiny, cluttered office in Royston. Walker usually had a case or two on
hand that he knew would pique the interest and exercise the
particular talents of his friend. This day was no exception.

"We've got a shooting death on our hands, Tom," said Walker,
leaning back in his chair. "Herb Lombard, the manager of a small
accounting firm in the Cummins Building, was found dead at his
desk late yesterday afternoon. He may have shot himself, but
we're not sure."

Stanwick idly fingered the tip of his mustache.

"Who discovered the body?" he asked.

"A client of his named John Morey, who works in another
office down the hall. Lombard was working on some late personal tax returns for him. Morey says he was leaving work yesterday,
shortly after five, when he passed the door of Lombard's firm and
decided to see if Lombard was in. The clerks had already left the
outer office, but light was shining from under the door of
Lombard's inner office.

"Morey knocked, opened the door, and found Lombard
slumped over his desk in a puddle of blood with a revolver in his
hand. Morey was so scared that, without touching anything in
the room, he ran down to a pay phone in the lobby and called
headquarters.

"I arrived a few minutes later and accompanied him back to
Lombard's inner office. Snapping on the light, I found everything
just as Morey had described. Lombard had been dead for less
than an hour, and had a bullet wound in his head. The revolver
had been fired once."

Stanwick shifted slightly in his chair.

"Poor devil," he remarked. "Did Morey find the door to the outer office open?"

"No, but it had been left unlocked," replied Walker.

"I see." Stanwick looked grim. "You'd better arrest Morey at once, Matt. He's lying about this affair!"

Why does Stanwick suspect Morey?

Solution on page 88.

The Case of the Purloined Painting
§

THERE WERE TIMES, thought Thomas P. Stanwick, when you could never count on having a friendly conversation without an interruption. Especially if your friend was a police inspector and you were visiting his office when a robbery call came in.

The amateur logician and Inspector Walker pulled up in front of a large brick house in a wealthy neighborhood in Royston and were quickly shown into the living room. A valuable painting had been stolen from the wall. The thief had apparently broken the glass in a nearby patio door, let himself in, and left by the same route. An obviously shaken maid was sitting in a large armchair when Stanwick and Walker entered.

"She discovered the theft and called it in, sir," a uniformed officer told Walker. "The couple who live here are out of town this week."

"What happened?" Walker asked the maid.

"I didn't hear a thing," she replied. "I had been working in the kitchen and was on my way to my room. When I passed the living room, I noticed that the painting was gone and that the glass in the patio door was broken. I called the police right away."

Stanwick carefully opened the patio door and walked out onto the concrete patio, stepping gingerly around the long shards of broken glass there as well as around any possible footmarks. He observed faint smudges of mud under the glass.

"How long had the painting hung in here?" he asked as he came back in.

"About two years, I guess," answered the maid.

Stanwick sat down in a comfortable armchair, crossed his legs, and turned to Walker.

"Well, Matt," he said, "I think you may want to ask this lady some more questions. This job involved inside help!"

Why is Stanwick sure that inside help was involved?

Solution on page 88.

The Week of the
Queen Anne Festival
§

A H, TO BE IN ENGLAND, now that summer's here, thought
Thomas P. Stanwick as he descended to the pub for breakfast. He was beginning a two-month vacation in England with a
week's stay at the Grey Boar Inn, a few miles outside Knordwyn.

The amateur logician had first visited Knordwyn, a tiny village in Northumbria, a year earlier, and had become very fond of
it and greatly intrigued by its peculiarities. Chief among these
was that about half the villagers always told the truth, and the
rest always lied. Stanwick thus found his conversations there
wonderful challenges for his powers of deduction.

It was a beautiful Monday morning, and Stanwick gathered
his thoughts over a hearty breakfast of eggs, bacon, toast, and
tea. He knew that this was the week of the Queen Anne
Festival, held annually in Knordwyn since Queen Anne stopped
overnight in the village on her way to visit Scotland in 1702.
People gathered on festival days from many surrounding towns to
enjoy dancing, balladeering, cooking, racing, and other activities.

The trouble was that the festival date and the number of festival days varied from year to year, and Stanwick wasn't sure
which days this year were the festival days. He knew that today
was not a festival day, and that the festival would be over before
Saturday. At least one, and possibly more, of the intervening
days would be festival days, and he wanted to know precisely
which.

Finishing his breakfast, Stanwick lit his pipe, leaned back in
his chair, and idly fingered a tip of his brown mustache as he
looked slowly around the room. The other tables were empty
except for one by a large window. Around that table were gathered three grizzled villagers, all cronies of the innkeeper, nursing

18

early mugs of ale. Stanwick had seen them before and knew that their names were Chiswick, Green, and Hunter, but he didn't know which were liars and which were truth-tellers. Well, he thought, perhaps today he would find out.

Stanwick arose and strolled over to their table.

"Good morning, gentlemen," he said cheerfully. "I beg your pardon, but could you please tell me which days this week are festival days? Also, if you'll excuse my asking, which of you are liars?"

The three villagers glanced at each other silently for a moment. Chiswick was the first to speak.

"We are all liars," said he, "and Friday is a festival day."

"He speaks the truth," Green said. "Also, Tuesday is a festival day."

Hunter took a gulp from his mug.

"If Chiswick is lying," he said as he set it down, "then Green is telling the truth. Also, Wednesday is a festival day."

"Thank you, gentlemen," said Stanwick, who turned and walked off with a delighted smile. He now knew which of the three were liars and which days that week were festival days.

Who is lying? Which days are festival days?
Solution on page 89.

Death of a Con Man
§

THOMAS P. STANWICK was engrossed in revising some notes at his desk late one spring afternoon when the doorbell rang. He opened the door and found Inspector Walker standing on the step.

"Matt! Come in," Stanwick exclaimed, stepping aside. "It's nice of you to drop by on your way back to Royston."

Walker looked surprised.

"How did you know which direction I came from?" he asked. "I parked in the driveway, not on the street."

"Quite so, but I observe that the small mud patch by the driveway entrance on the side toward Royston is undisturbed. Had you come from Royston, you could hardly have avoided at least grazing it as you turned in."

Walker laughed as they settled themselves into a pair of comfortable armchairs in the living room.

"Never expect to keep secrets when you visit a logician," he said. "I'm on my way back from Richford, where I've been following up some leads on the Edmunds murder last week."

"Edmunds? Isn't he the con man who was shot in a shipping warehouse?" asked Stanwick as he relit his pipe.

"That's right. We've arrested four members of a gang he recently fleeced: Cannon, Cochran, Carruthers, and Carpenter. We know one of them is the killer. Our polygraph showed that each made one true statement and one false statement this morning under interrogation, but we couldn't determine which was which."

Stanwick leaned forward eagerly. "Do you have a copy of the statements?"

Walker smiled, reached into his coat pocket, and pulled out a folded document.

"I thought you might find them interesting," he said as he

handed the paper across. "If you can make any use of them, I'd be glad to hear your conclusions."

Stanwick unfolded the paper, leaned back, and read:

> Cannon: I did not kill Edmunds. Carpenter is the killer.
>
> Cochran: I did not kill Edmunds. Cannon is lying when he says Carpenter is the killer.
>
> Carruthers: I did not kill Edmunds. Either Cannon is the killer or none of us is.
>
> Carpenter: I did not kill Edmunds. If Carruthers did not kill Edmunds, then Cannon did.

"At least they were all consistent with their denials," Stanwick said with a laugh. "However, a little deduction is enough to clear up the matter. The killer is…"

Who is the killer?

Solution on page 89.

The Case of the
Edgemore Street Shooting
§

"THANKS FOR COMING over, Tom," said Inspector Matt Walker as Thomas P. Stanwick, the amateur logician, strolled into the inspector's office at Royston Police headquarters.

"Glad to," Stanwick replied as he flopped into a chair. "You said you were going to interrogate a suspect in that recent street shooting."

"That's right." Walker lit a cheap cigar. "As you may already know, Bruce Walder, a local businessman in his mid-fifties, was walking along Edgemore Street about dusk two days ago. Someone approached him, shot him in the chest, and ran off. We suspect that the shooter wanted to rob him, and shot him when Walder started to resist.

"We haven't located anyone who actually saw the crime, but several locals were able to describe a man they saw lounging in the street shortly before it took place. Their descriptions matched that of Victor Kravitz, a small-time mugger known to frequent the area. We picked up Kravitz just a few hours ago. Let's hear what he has to say."

They went to a nearby interrogation room. Kravitz, a small, nervous man with thinning blond hair, sat beside his lawyer and chain-smoked. Two detectives leaned against the wall while Walker and Stanwick sat down at the table.

"You've got it all wrong," cried Kravitz. "I didn't shoot Walder. I was on the street earlier, sure, but just hanging around. When I saw some guy come out of an alley, come up behind the stiff, and shoot him, I ran. I didn't want no trouble."

"You saw the crime committed?" asked Walker.

"Yeah. Yeah."

"Why didn't you report it?" asked one of the other detectives.

Kravitz laughed nervously. "Sure. Like you guys were about to believe me."

"Can you describe the man?" Walker inquired.

"Sure, sure. Middle-aged guy, tall, red mustache. Wore a big gray overcoat and a hat. Walder never even saw him."

"Where did you run to?"

"My girlfriend's place. You can ask her."

Stanwick, who had been slouching back in his chair, cleared his throat and slowly sat up.

"I for one have heard enough, Matt," he said to Walker. "This man is obviously lying."

How does Stanwick know that Kravitz is lying?

Solution on page 89.

Death Comes to the Colonel
§

THOMAS P. STANWICK, the amateur logician, and Inspector Matthew Walker of the Royston Police strode into the richly carpeted study of Jeremy Huddleston. It was a chilly Tuesday in late fall, and Stanwick had been chatting in Walker's office when word came in of Huddleston's sudden death. Poisoning was suspected.

Huddleston, a retired army colonel in his seventies, lay behind his desk in the middle of the room, partly covered by his overturned chair. His sightless eyes stared at the ceiling as a fire crackled in the large brick hearth behind the desk. Near the hearth, a young, balding man sat wearily in an armchair. Walker approached him.

"Mr. Huddleston?" he asked. "Mr. George Huddleston?"

The young man nodded.

"The colonel's grand-nephew, aren't you?"

"Yes."

"Please tell us what happened."

Huddleston looked up nervously and wet his lips. "I came into the study about ten this morning to say good morning to Uncle Jeremy. He was working at his desk and seemed to be in cheerful spirits. He asked me to pour him another cup of coffee from the sideboard, so I did. He drank about half of it, and then suddenly put his cup down and said, 'Before I forget, I must call Phillips to fix the leak in the basement pipes.'"

"Roy Phillips, the local plumber?" Walker cut in.

"That's right." Huddleston continued. "He had just started to dial his private phone when he uttered a sharp cry, clutched suddenly at his throat, and fell over onto the floor. I was horrified and rushed over to him, but could see at once that he was dead.

"Hurrying out to the hall, I locked the study door and called to his housekeeper, Mrs. Stowe, who phoned the doctor and the police. I kept the study door locked until you arrived."

A medical assistant touched Walker on the shoulder.

"Excuse me, sir," he said. "The drops we extracted from the coffee cup show definite traces of cyanide."

Walker nodded. Stanwick lit his pipe and looked slowly around the room. His gaze rested in turn on the cheery fire warming the room of death, on the half-empty coffee cup resting neatly in its saucer, and on the West Point ring adorning the victim's finger.

"Do you live here, Mr. Huddleston?" Stanwick asked, suddenly turning to the nephew.

"No," replied Huddleston. "I live in California, where I work for an architectural firm. I was here only for the week, to visit Uncle Jeremy and see the East Coast again."

The phone on the colonel's desk rang. Walker answered it and bluntly told the caller, an old friend of the colonel's nephew, that the colonel was dead and a police investigation was in progress. After hanging up, he faced George Huddleston again.

"What more can you tell us, Mr. Huddleston?" he asked.

"Nothing," replied Huddleston listlessly.

"On the contrary," said Stanwick sharply, "I think Mr. Huddleston could help by telling us the truth."

How does Stanwick know that Huddleston is lying?

Solution on page 89.

Stanwick Finds the
Magic Words

§

THE SMALL DOWNTOWN SECTION of Baskerville was unusually busy that Saturday morning. After browsing through several other stores, Thomas P. Stanwick wandered into the Baskerville Bookshop, a crowded, bright little store displaying books, greeting cards and, in a far corner, toys. He was looking for a birthday present for the younger son of his friend Inspector Matt Walker. Tim Walker was about to turn six.

Weaving his way through knots of other customers, Stanwick made his way to the toy corner. There he spotted a toy he knew Tim would love: a bright red fire truck. Scooping it up, Stanwick started for the checkout counter and then stopped with a sudden realization. He had accidentally left his wallet at home.

With a sigh of annoyance, Stanwick turned to put the truck back. As he did, he saw a sign near a collection of puzzle books:

SAY THE MAGIC WORDS!

How sharp are your puzzle skills? Tell us the logical conclusion of the following statements and win the book or toy of your choice!

1. All friends of winged armadillos wear striped ties.

2. Only those who eat pickled harmonicas can enter a chocolate courtroom.

3. Members of the Diagonal Club drink martinis only at four.

4. All who eat pickled harmonicas are friends of winged armadillos.

5. Only those green elephants who are members of the Diagonal Club can wear striped ties.

6. All green elephants drink martinis at five.

Stanwick's eyes sparkled. For a few moments, he stood stock still, staring at the sign and fingering the tip of his mustache. Then, with a gesture of triumph, he swung the truck back under his arm, strode to the checkout counter, and won the truck for Tim by saying the magic words.

What are the magic words?

Solution on page 90.

The Great Watermelon Cover-Up

§

THOMAS P. STANWICK had just stepped into Kreckman's Grocery Store in Baskerville to buy some tea and some pipe tobacco when the owner, Otto Kreckman, hurried up to him anxiously.

"Mr. Stanwick, I'm so glad to see you," he said. "Come see what's happened!"

Kreckman led Stanwick down an aisle of the small shop. At the far end, several large watermelons had been knocked from a display table and lay smashed on the floor. Four ten-year-old boys stood nervously around the pulpy wreckage.

"These boys were fooling around back here," said the grocer angrily, "and one or more of them knocked over my melons. None will admit doing it, though.

"The damage isn't much," he told Stanwick privately in a lower voice, "but whoever is guilty should learn some responsibility."

Stanwick, affecting a cold stare, silently looked from one boy to the next as he slowly filled and lit his pipe. They all lived in Baskerville, and he knew their names.

"Richard," he asked abruptly, "who knocked over those melons?"

"Harry and Frank knocked them over," Richard replied.

Harry and Frank angrily turned to him.

"I didn't knock them over!" said Frank hotly.

Stanwick turned to the redheaded boy. "What do you have to say, Tommy?"

Tommy fidgeted uncomfortably. "Only one of us knocked the melons over."

"How about you, Harry?"

"What Tommy and Frank said is true," Harry replied sullenly.

Kreckman took Stanwick aside.

"They won't tell me any more than that," said the grocer. "Now, I know these boys. Tommy's an honest kid, and I'm sure he wouldn't lie to me. He's too loyal to his friends to tell me who's responsible, though.

"Harry, on the other hand, is a different sort altogether and lies his head off anytime he's suspected of mischief. As for the others, I don't know whom to believe, and I can't pinpoint the culprits."

"In that case," said Stanwick with a sly smile, "I can be of some help. I know exactly who is responsible."

Who knocked over the watermelons?

Solution on page 90.

Inspector Walker
Feels the Heat
§

"HELLO, TOM? MATT HERE. Have you got a few minutes to spare this afternoon? We're really up against it here, and I could use some advice. Mind if I come right over? Thanks."

As Thomas P. Stanwick hung up the phone, he reflected that his friend Inspector Walker, who had just called from police headquarters, sounded unusually tense and anxious. A few prominent citizens of the city of Royston had been assaulted recently, and Stanwick wondered if one of those cases might be troubling Walker.

Within half an hour, the inspector had driven out from Royston and arrived at Stanwick's bungalow in Baskerville. The amateur logician promptly ushered him into the living room, where they sat down.

"You look pretty harried, Matt," observed Stanwick as he filled his pipe. "What's up?"

"It's the attack on the deputy mayor two nights ago," Walker replied.

"Ah, yes. I remember reading something about it in the paper. Beaten and robbed as he walked home after attending a late neighborhood committee meeting, I think."

"That's right. He wasn't very badly hurt, but is still in the hospital. The night was so dark, and the attack so sudden, that he isn't sure whether he was attacked by one man or several. The mayor has ordered an all-out investigation, and has really turned on the pressure."

Stanwick grinned faintly. "I can imagine."

"Our search," continued Walker, "has narrowed down to five men. One is Robert Ellis, a small-time mugger. The other four are a gang of ruffians from the north end of the city. Their names are Al Chase, Archie Heath, Dick Mullaney, and Bull Decker. At least one of the five is guilty."

"What can you tell me about them?"

Walker took out his notebook.

"We've spent the last two days," he said, "checking the activities of the gang members that night. So far, we've learned only enough to be sure of the following:

"1. If Chase is guilty and Heath is innocent, then Decker is guilty.

"2. If Chase is innocent, then Mullaney is innocent.

"3. If Heath is guilty, then Mullaney is guilty.

"4. Chase and Heath are not both guilty.

"5. Unless Heath is guilty, Decker is innocent.

"That's all of it, Tom. Not many hard facts, I'm afraid. The heat is really on, though, so if you can deduce anything more from what we have, I'll be very grateful."

Stanwick accepted the notebook and studied its scribbled entries with complete absorption. Walker, still agitated and restless, got up and paced the floor.

A few moments later, Stanwick closed the notebook and looked up with a smile.

"Well, Matt," he said cheerfully, "it's about time you relaxed. You've given me enough to determine who is guilty and who is innocent in this matter."

Who assaulted the deputy mayor?
Solution on page 90.

INSPECTOR WALKER

Stanwick Visits Scotland Yard
§

"STANWICK, MY DEAR FELLOW," exclaimed Bodwin, "you couldn't possibly have chosen a better moment to come to London."

"London in April hasn't quite the reputation of the French capital," replied Thomas P. Stanwick with a grin as he sat down. "Still, I'm always glad to be back."

The amateur logician had stopped at Scotland Yard to visit his old friend Inspector Gilbert Bodwin. Stanwick was in London for a week to attend a Churchill Society dinner in Pall Mall.

"I expect this must be a particularly busy time for you," Stanwick continued, "with the foreign ministers' conference only a week away."

Bodwin leaned forward intently across his desk. "It is indeed, and that's why I'm glad to have a chance to talk with you."

"Oh?" Stanwick finished lighting his pipe and peered at Bodwin curiously through a cloud of smoke.

"Yes, and the Prime Minister is furious at the breach in security. Some important state papers were taken from a safe at the Foreign and Commonwealth Office two nights ago, at about nine-thirty. From the way it was done, we know the thief had to have known the combination of the safe.

"We have three suspects. They are all clerks in the FCO: James Malcolm, Samuel Hickory, and William Dell. Each knows the combination as part of his duties."

Stanwick, full of interest, absentmindedly fingered a tip of his mustache.

"Of course you've questioned them," he said. "Just what accounts do they give of their whereabouts on the evening of the theft?"

Bodwin flipped open a notebook. "Malcolm says he went to the theatre with his wife that evening. "

The inspector produced four scraps of paper, which Stanwick recognized as the halves of two torn tickets.

"He showed us these from his jacket pocket," Bodwin went on. "As you can see, they are for that evening's 8:00 o'clock performance of 'Coningsby' at the Disraeli Playhouse in Southwark. The play lasted until ten, and the ushers say no one left early. The Malcolms live in Chiswick and say they travelled to and from the theatre in their own car.

"Hickory maintains that he was engrossed in a darts tournament at his neighborhood pub from eight until eleven that night. That's the Sacred Cow in St. John's Wood. I have statements here from several of the

33

regulars, all of whom confirm that Hickory was there the whole time."

"Does he often play darts there?" asked Stanwick.

"The regulars say he stops by about twice a week for an evening pint," Bodwin replied, "but he hardly ever plays darts."

"How about Dell?"

"He's the only one without an alibi that we could readily verify. He lives alone and says he spent the whole evening watching television. He told my sergeant the plots of all that evening's BBC1 programs, but he's still our prime suspect. There just isn't anything solid to go on."

"Does he also live in town?"

Bodwin nodded. "Small flat in Belgrave Road. Any suggestions? The P. M. will want my head on a platter if we don't nab our man."

Stanwick laughed and languidly stood up.

"I'm ready for a bite of lunch," he said. "If you'll join me in a stroll to the little pub I saw down the street, I'll be glad to tell you the identity of the thief."

Who stole the documents?

Solution on page 90.

The Explorer's Tale
§

THOMAS P. STANWICK, the amateur logician, had seldom been so surprised or delighted. In return for what he considered a few trifling deductions that had helped avert the disruption of an important state conference in London, the Queen had given him free passage back to the United States aboard a luxury passenger liner.

Stanwick quickly fell into the routine on board and began to enjoy the cruise thoroughly. By day he strode the deck, read, played games, or leaned against the railing and gazed out at the dark waters of the North Atlantic. By night he dined in elegance with the other passengers and then relaxed in one of the ship's lounges, engrossed in conversation, chess, cards, or a good book.

On the evening of the sixth day, Stanwick was sitting in a comfortable armchair and listening to a long travelogue by Gregory Justin, a self-proclaimed adventurer and explorer. Justin, a stout, middle-aged man with a ruddy face and thinning red hair, leaned toward Stanwick and spoke with obvious relish.

"Later that year," he went on, "I led an expedition of 20 on a photographic tour of the jungles and plains of Zambia. We were there almost three months, and what a time we had! The jungles were dark and beautiful but safe enough, as long as we were careful about the occasional snake or tiger that crossed our path. On the plain, though, we once had a pretty harrowing night.

"We had spent that day photographing an elephant herd and a pride of lions. The male lions slept most of the day, but when they shook their great manes and looked up, they were a magnificent sight.

"We made camp that night on the plain, about two miles from the pride. At two-thirty, I was awakened by some yelling. A rogue lioness with a dangerous appetite had found our camp and was clawing at some of the tents. I looked out and could see her in the moonlight, so I grabbed my rifle, got her in my sights, and put her down. I hated to do it, but it was necessary."

"You had quite an exciting time, I guess," remarked Stanwick with a smile. He arose lazily and shook hands with Justin. "Thank you. I enjoyed your stories. I have some letters to write this evening, so I'll now wish you a good night."

Before returning to his cabin, Stanwick stepped out on deck and strolled to the railing. A few sparks from his pipe danced out into the inky void.

"Justin's a fine storyteller," he muttered to himself. "It's a pity his stories aren't entirely true!"

What flaw did Stanwick find in Justin's story?

Solution on page 90.

The Case of the
Reindeer Spies
§

THE RINGING OF THE doorbell cut through the clacking of the keyboard in Thomas P. Stanwick's small study. The amateur logician arose from the history textbook he was editing and went to the door. Rufus, his black labrador, lifted his head sleepily from his paws.

"Mr. Stanwick?" A tall man in a brown suit flashed a badge. "I'm Special Agent Stevens of the F.B.I. Inspector Walker of the Royston Police referred me to you. Do you mind if I come in?"

"Not at all." Though surprised by the visit, Stanwick showed Stevens into the living room with quiet geniality. It was not the first time that he had received unusual visitors through Walker's recommendations.

Stevens glanced curiously around at the crowded bookshelves, the wall maps, and the papers and dusty chess sets piled on various side tables. Declining Stanwick's offer of tea, he seated himself in an armchair near the hearth. Stanwick sat down in an armchair across from him and relit his pipe.

"Matt Walker is a good friend of mine, Mr. Stevens," he said, "and I'm always glad to help him or an associate of his if I can. I presume that in this case I may be of some service to the government."

"Exactly, Mr. Stanwick," replied Stevens. "I've come to you because this case has a tangled knot of facts, and Walker says you can untangle such knots better than anyone else he knows. We are also aware, of course, of your past services to the American and British governments.

"Briefly, the facts are these. As a result of the national effort to crack down on domestic spies, the Bureau has uncovered a ring of five spies in Royston who have started selling defense industry secrets to the Chinese consulate in New York. The five individuals have been identified, and we are intercepting their messages.

"We believe they may be able to lead us to several similar rings in the Midwest, so we want to continue monitoring their messages a while longer before we arrest them. Our problem is that they refer to each other in code names, and we need to match the individuals to the code names before we can completely understand the messages."

Stanwick reached lazily for a pad of paper and a pencil. "What do you have so far?" he asked.

Stevens opened a notebook.

"The code names," he said with a slight smile, "are those of well-known reindeer: Comet, Cupid, Dasher, Dancer, and Donder. We are certain that these names correspond in some order to the members of the group, all of whom live in Royston.

"Sal Abelardo is a civil engineer for Spacetech. His wife works for a publishing company and apparently knows nothing of his espionage activities. Peter Bircham works as a janitor for the same firm. He is single. John Cantrell is a junior executive with Aeroco. He and his wife share a condo downtown with his sister. Tim Delmarin, unmarried, is a communications expert with the same firm. The fifth member is Telly Ephesos, a retired Foreign Service Officer who spent twenty years in China. He is married and has no siblings."

Stanwick puffed on his pipe and wrote quietly on the pad, while Rufus delicately sniffed the visitor's briefcase.

"From the messages already sent," continued Stevens, "and our own investigation, we've been able to glean only a few facts. Cantrell and 'Dasher' and their wives sometimes take vacations together. 'Cupid' is highly dissatisfied with his job. Mrs. Abelardo regularly corresponds with 'Mrs. Donder.' Neither 'Comet' nor 'Dasher' has ever been outside the state. Mrs. Abelardo was once engaged to the brother of 'Donder.' Finally, Bircham makes monthly trips to Mexico City.

"I cannot impress upon you enough, Mr. Stanwick, the importance of identifying these code names. Any help you could give us in this matter would be greatly appreciated."

Stanwick, too preoccupied to answer immediately, paused and fingered a tip of his mustache as languid wisps of smoke curled up from his pipe. A moment later he scribbled something on his pad and tossed it to Stevens.

"Here are the code names and their possessors. Happy hunting!"

Who has which code name?

Solution on pages 90–91.

Stanwick and the
Accidental Thief

§

THOMAS P. STANWICK roamed the Christmas-lit aisles of Schweppe's Department Store, looking for the right gift for his old friend Annie Tynsdale. Annie owned a candy shop in Cambridge, England.

The women's accessories aisle seemed safe enough. He strolled down it slowly, eying successive displays of purses, handkerchiefs, wallets, coin purses, scarves, and gloves. Though the prices on the tags were unexpectedly high, the goods were all handsome and of good quality. He paused by the glove table and picked up a pair.

Just then a small commotion at the front of the store attracted his attention. Jim Sperlich, the store detective, had just re-entered the store grasping a young blond woman firmly by the arm. In his other hand he held a brown leather coin purse. The woman, her face flushed, struggled to free her arm.

"Let me go, you gorilla," she spat. "I was going to pay for it!"

"We'll let the store manager decide," Sperlich replied stolidly. "Just come along, please." He guided her toward a small office in the back of the store.

Stanwick, who knew both Sperlich and the store manager, Dale Carpenter, decided to be on hand. Putting down the gloves, he strode to Carpenter's office, which was closer to him than to Sperlich and his captive.

"Merry Christmas, Dale!" he exclaimed to Carpenter, who looked up from his papers with a start. "How's business these days?"

"Hello, Tom! Why, it's not too —"

"Excuse me, Mr. Carpenter." Sperlich arrived with the woman, and Stanwick smiled and smoothly stepped to a corner of the office. "Hi, Tom. I caught this lady shoplifting, Mr. Carpenter. I spotted her just as she was thrusting this coin purse into her jacket pocket, and stayed near her until she left the premises without paying for it. Then I apprehended her."

"It's all an innocent mistake!" exclaimed the woman, wrench-

ing her arm free at last and facing Carpenter angrily. "I intended to pay for it. I'm just absent-minded, and forgot at the last minute that I had it."

Carpenter took the coin purse and quickly examined its leather exterior. Snapping it open, he checked the lining and extracted the price tag.

"One of our better brands of ladies' coin purses," he noted. "May I ask, Ms. —"

"Leonard. Celia Leonard."

"May I ask, Ms. Leonard, why you put this purse in your pocket?"

"I tucked it away—temporarily—because I wanted to try on a few pairs of gloves, and so needed to free my hands." She turned angrily to Sperlich. "Isn't that right, Mr. Hot Shot Detective? If you were staying so close to me, you must have seen me try on the gloves."

Sperlich's face flushed a little.

"Well, it's true, Mr. Carpenter," he replied. "After putting the purse in her pocket, she did try on three or four pairs of gloves. And put them all back."

"See there?" She smiled at the manager in cold triumph. "Now please let me pay for or return the coin purse and be on my way."

Carpenter scratched his balding head. "Well, I don't know. Technically, of course, you are guilty of shoplifting by leaving the store without paying for the item, whether or not you intended to do so. However, since there seems to be good reason to believe that it wasn't intentional, maybe —"

"Just a moment, Dale." Stanwick interrupted him and stepped forward. "This lady's theft of the coin purse was quite intentional, and I think you should press charges."

How does Stanwick know that she intended to steal the purse?

Solution on page 91.

The McPherson–McTavish Mystery

§

EARLY ONE DRIZZLY MORNING, as Thomas P. Stanwick was finishing breakfast at the White Lion Inn, the innkeeper told him he was wanted on the phone. This surprised him, since he was on the third day of a vacation in Dartmoor, England, and few people knew he was there.

"Mr. Stanwick? This is Inspector Carstairs," said the voice on the phone.

"Oh, yes." The amateur logician had met the inspector at the local pub two days earlier and had swapped crime stories with him. "What can I do for you?"

"Colonel Rogers was murdered in his library last evening. Since you've been helpful in other police investigations, I thought you might be interested in dropping by and having a look at this one."

"Thank you, Carstairs, I'd be delighted."

The Rogers estate was only two miles across the moor from the inn, so within an hour Stanwick had walked to the main house, scraped the sticky red clay of the moor from his feet, and joined Carstairs in the library. Colonel Rogers lay in front of his desk, shot in the chest at point-blank range.

Carstairs pointed to two grizzled, middle-aged men sitting sullenly nearby.

"That's McTavish on the right and McPherson on the left. McTavish is a neighbor and McPherson is the groundskeeper here. McTavish says he saw McPherson bury the murder weapon, a shotgun, in the garden last evening."

"That's right, sir," cried McTavish. "I had my telescope set up just a few miles away on a little knoll on the moor. Before lookin' out at the stars, I swung it around the landscape a bit—to test it,

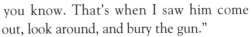

you know. That's when I saw him come out, look around, and bury the gun."

"A rotten lie!" roared McPherson. "I was in my cottage all evening until the constable came knocking last night."

"That's enough!" Carstairs warned. "We dug up that shotgun last night from the spot in the garden that McTavish showed us. All indications are that it's the murder weapon."

Stanwick examined the dirty shotgun leaning against the wall. Beside the shotgun was a golf bag with a broken strap, scuffed along the bottom but otherwise unmarked. Inside, however, Stanwick found no clubs, but telescopic equipment instead.

"Is this your golf bag, Mr. McTavish?" he asked.

"Aye. Every week for months now, I've dragged that bag with my telescope from the village up to the knoll to look at the stars."

"Wasn't it too cloudy last night for that?"

"No, it rained a bit in the afternoon, but by dusk it had cleared some."

"How could you see Mr. McPherson at night?"

"Oh, at dusk it was still light enough to see what he was doin'."

Stanwick sat down in a nearby armchair and fingered the tip of his mustache.

Mr. McPherson," he asked, "did you hear a shot last night?"

"No, sir," was the reply. "My cottage is some distance from the library."

"Who called you, Carstairs?"

"I received a call from McTavish, who said he had just rushed back to the village. We picked him up with his equipment, came here, discovered the body, and found the gun where he said McPherson had buried it."

"Any fingerprints?"

"None left on the gun, and only those of the colonel in the room. Also, the housekeeper tells me an ivory-handled knife is missing from his desk."

"Well, well." Stanwick abruptly arose and faced McTavish. "I think you had better start telling the truth, Mr. McTavish. Your story is a lie!"

How does Stanwick know McTavish is lying?

Solution on page 91.

Murder in a London Flat

§

L ORD CALINORE WAS GUNNED down in his London flat by a
robber, who then ransacked the flat. The case was placed in
the capable hands of Inspector Gilbert Bodwin of Scotland Yard.
Bodwin's investigation revealed that one man had planned the
crime, another had carried it out, and a third had acted as lookout.

Bodwin discussed the case at length one evening over dinner
at his club with an old friend, Thomas P. Stanwick, the amateur
logician, visiting from America.

"It's quite a case," Stanwick remarked. "Have you any suspects?"

Bodwin sliced his roast beef with relish. "Yes, indeed. Four. We
have conclusive evidence that three of those four were responsible for the crime."

"Really! That's remarkable progress. What about the fourth?"

"He had no prior knowledge of the crime and is completely
innocent. The problem is that we're not sure which of the four
are the planner, the gunman, the lookout, and the innocent
bystander."

"I see." Stanwick took more Yorkshire pudding. "What do you
know about them at this point?"

"Well, the names of the four are Merrick, Cross, Llewellyn,
and Halifax. Halifax and Cross play golf together every Saturday.
They're an odd pair! Halifax can't drive, and Cross has been out
of Dartmoor Prison for only a year."

"What was he in for?"

"Forgery. We know that Merrick and Halifax kept the flat
under surveillance for several days just before the day the crime
was committed, the 17th. Llewellyn and Merrick, with their
wives, had dinner together on the Strand on the 12th."

"An interesting compilation," said Stanwick, "but hardly conclusive. Is that all of it?"

"Not quite. We know that the gunman spent the week before the crime in Edinburgh, and that the innocent bystander was acquainted with the planner and the gunman, but not with the lookout."

"That is very helpful," said Stanwick with a smile. He raised his wine glass. "Bodwin, old fellow, your case is complete."

Who are the planner, the gunman, and the lookout?

Solution on page 91.

The Road to Trigoon
§

IT WAS AUGUST IN the Scottish Highlands, and Thomas P. Stanwick, the amateur logician, strode happily along the road. He was well along on a hundred-mile walking holiday, and the exercise had invigorated his lanky but usually sedentary frame. Three days more would see him to Cape Wrath and the end of his journey.

Stanwick was passing through an isolated and little-known area of the Highlands inhabited exclusively by members of two clans, the MacDurgalls and the MacFurbishes. They had lived there for many centuries, and abided by time-honored customs. The oldest of these was that the MacDurgalls always told the truth and the MacFurbishes always lied. The origin of this peculiar tradition was long forgotten, but the tradition itself was rigorously observed.

Stanwick intended to stay the night in Trigoon, a village in a distant glen. His map of the region, however, was sketchy. As he rounded a bend, admiring the verdant hills around him, he came upon an unexpected fork in the road.

No direction sign was to be seen. Fortunately, three inhabitants of the region were sitting by the wayside, eating their lunches after working in a nearby field. Stanwick approached them.

"Excuse me," he said, "but which of these is the road to Trigoon?"

"The road on the right," replied the first man.

"The road on the left," said the second man.

"Either road is fine," said the third man.

The first man jumped up angrily and faced the second man. "You're lying!" he roared.

"No, you are!" said the second man, coming to his feet.

The third man also came to his feet. "Bruce speaks the truth!"

48

he said angrily to the first man.

The three of them continued arguing fiercely among themselves. Stanwick smiled, murmured his thanks, and set off along the road to Trigoon.

Which is the road to Trigoon?

Solution on page 91.

The Matter of the
McAlister Murders
§

WHIT KNOWLTON, A RETIRED lawyer in his eighties, loved to reminisce about his trials. His memory was shaky, however, and he sometimes had to let his listeners fill in blank spots in his narrative.

One lazy Sunday afternoon in the summer, Knowlton was sitting in his well-stocked library swapping stories with Thomas P. Stanwick. The amateur logician always enjoyed his visits with Knowlton.

"The McAlister murders in Baltimore hit the papers in the winter of 1953," said the lawyer. "Four men were arrested for the murders within a week, and I was called in to assist the district attorney.

"All four were indicted, but evidence brought out in the course of the trial proved that only two of them were guilty. Our problem was to find out which two they were."

"How useful was their testimony?" asked Stanwick.

"Oh, useful enough, as it turned out," Knowlton replied. "The first defendant, Addler, said that either the second defendant, Byran, was guilty, or the fourth defendant, Derrick, was innocent. Byran said that he was innocent, and that either Addler or Collins, the third defendant, was guilty.

"Collins said that Byran and Derrick were not both guilty. Derrick, after a long refusal to speak at all, said that Collins was innocent if and only if Addler was also innocent."

"Were any of their statements proven true?" Stanwick asked.

"Well, yes. Other evidence proved that the two guilty ones were lying and the two innocent ones were telling the truth. Unfortunately, I don't quite remember anymore who the guilty ones were."

Stanwick smiled and fumbled in his pocket for his pipe.

"This case is a treat, Whit," he said, "for it's not too hard to deduce who the guilty ones were."

Who were the guilty ones?

Solution on page 92.

Death in the Garage
§

INSPECTOR MATTHEW WALKER AND Thomas P. Stanwick had barely begun their weekly game that Thursday evening at the chess club when Walker's beeper went off.

"There's been a suspicious death in Caterina Road," said Walker when he returned from the phone. "Probably a suicide. Care to come?"

"By all means. Some evenings weren't made for chess."

A quarter of an hour later, Walker and Stanwick were in the garage of Walter McCarthy, a real estate broker. McCarthy was seated behind the wheel of his car, dead. The garage door was open, the car was silent, and the police were busily at work.

"The body was discovered by Mrs. McCarthy when she returned home on foot about six," reported Sergeant Hatch. "The car was running. Nearly overcome by exhaust fumes herself, she opened the garage door from the inside, switched off the car, and called 9-1-1 from the kitchen. She's inside now."

"Cause of death established?" asked Walker.

"The medical examiner says the body shows every sign of carbon monoxide asphyxiation. We did find these in the right jacket pocket, though." Hatch handed Walker a plastic evidence bag containing a pill bottle. Walker gingerly removed the bottle, glanced at the label, and popped open the cap. The bottle was half full of large, pink lozenges.

"A prescription depressant," he remarked. "Refilled only yesterday for one pill a day, and yet half the pills are gone. Could these have killed him?"

"No, they couldn't," responded Dr. Pillsbury, the owlish medical examiner, who now approached Walker. "If he took half the bottle, though, the dose would have knocked him out in about fifteen seconds."

"But why would he take the pills if he were about to asphyxiate himself anyway?" asked Stanwick. "Asphyxiation is painless."

Pillsbury shrugged. "It is. But he may have wanted to put himself under sooner, before he could lose his nerve. I've seen it before in suicides."

"Hatch," said Walker, turning to the sergeant, "what was found in the car?"

"Nothing unusual, sir. Registration, maps, ice scraper, a scarf, a bag of chips. A folder of house listings. In the trunk, some tools, a spare, jumper cables, a blanket."

"Has a suicide note turned up?"

"Not yet, sir. We're still checking the house."

"And how much gas was in the tank?" asked Stanwick.

"Oh, plenty, sir. More than enough."

"Thank you, sergeant," said Walker. "Please tell Mrs. McCarthy I'll see her soon."

"Yes, sir."

As Hatch strode off, Walker turned back to Stanwick.

"Well, Tom, I'm afraid there's not much of special interest here. Whether or not we find a note, this looks to me like a straightforward suicide."

Stanwick shook his head solemnly.

"I don't think so, Matt," he replied. "Though I can't be certain, I think this is a case of murder."

Why does Stanwick think McCarthy was murdered?

Solution on page 92.

Murder at the Chessboard
§

Thomas P. Stanwick and Inspector Matthew Walker were
seated one afternoon in Stanwick's living room, chatting
about recent crime news.

"You may have seen something in the papers," said Walker,
"about the murder two nights ago of Professor Richard
Hansford."

"Yes, I think so." Stanwick frowned. "The archaeologist. He
was stabbed in the back while seated at a chessboard in his
study, wasn't he? Killed instantly."

"That's right. A call came in to headquarters at 8:30 last
Wednesday night from Michael Rimbach, a visiting relative of
Hansford's.

"When the squad car arrived, Rimbach explained to the officers that he had heard a cry from the study as he was passing by
in the hallway. Looking in, he saw the professor slumped back in
his chair and caught a glimpse of a man escaping through the
French doors of the study onto the lawn. Rimbach rushed to the
doors, but the man had already disappeared into the rainy dark-
ness.

"Hansford was obviously dead, so without touching anything,
Rimbach called the police and told Hansford's sister Emily of the
crime. Emily, an invalid, had heard nothing.

"Rimbach thinks he recognized the man as David Kunst, a
neighbor who played chess with Hansford every Wednesday
evening at 7:30. They were both enthusiasts of monochromatic
chess, and played no other kind."

"Really?" said Stanwick. "Chess in which no piece can move
from a black square to a white square, or vice versa? That's quite
rare."

"Yes, it is, which is why they played it so regularly. It's hard to
find partners for it. Rimbach, the sister, and Kunst all confirmed

the weekly games.

"When we interviewed Kunst at his home later that evening," Walker continued, "he said he had received a call from Rimbach a little after seven saying that Hansford was ill and had to cancel that evening's game. Kunst said he therefore spent the evening at home. Rimbach denies having called him. Kunst lives alone, and there were no witnesses. We saw a damp overcoat and shoes there, but he says they got wet on his way home from work."

"In what condition did you find the study?" Stanwick asked.

"The French doors were open. We looked for footprint traces on the lawn, but found nothing definite. The condition of the board indicated that a game was in progress when the murder occurred."

"Did the board look like the game had been in progress for an hour?"

"Yes, I guess so. It looked like the players were entering the middle part of the game. A knight and two bishops were already posted in the center of the board."

"Had the weekly game ever been called off before?"

"Now and then. Usually the sister phoned Kunst if Hansford was ill. She had been confined to her bed that day, though, and hadn't seen her brother."

"Well," said Stanwick, fingering the tip of his mustache, "you have an interesting but thoroughly contradictory pair of stories to consider. One of them is patently untrue, however, so I suggest you concentrate your inquiry in the direction of the liar."

Who is lying?

Solution on page 92.

The Norfolk Bank Robbery
§

THOMAS P. STANWICK, the amateur logician, was a familiar and welcome visitor at Royston Police headquarters. Shortly after noon on a fine Tuesday in spring, he returned a nod to the duty sergeant and strolled to the office of Inspector Matt Walker.

"The Ides of April are almost upon us, my lad," said Stanwick cheerily. Walker looked up from the piles of papers on his desk with a weary smile.

"Tax time! Don't remind me," he said. "It's good to see you though, Tom."

"What's been happening?" Stanwick began to fill his pipe.

"How about a bank robbery?"

"A bank robbery!" Stanwick laughed. "Isn't that a bit old-fashioned, what with electronic transfers and all? I suppose you'll be investigating a stagecoach holdup next."

"You'd be surprised, Tom," Walker replied. "Banks still handle quite a lot of actual cash, and that still attracts the bad guys."

"Indeed!," said Stanwick, arching his eyebrows. "What bank got held up?"

"Last Friday, about two o'clock," related Walker, "two men wearing Halloween masks entered the Norfolk Bank and Trust and demanded the money in the teller cages and in the safe. One man kept a gun drawn while the other collected the cash in a burlap sack. During some last-minute confusion, the gunman shot a teller. Luckily, she'll be all right. The two made off with about $77,000 and were driven from the scene by a third man in a blue Toyota."

Stanwick grunted. "What have you found out since then?"

"A good deal." Walker leaned forward intently. "We got a partial license number off the car, and have been canvassing our street informants. We're now convinced that the three belong to a small syndicate composed of five men: Howard Kuhlman,

Thomas Brinner, Will Langley, George Pickett, and Fred Schartner. We don't know much about them, but so far have been able to assemble the following facts:

"1. Kuhlman and the shooter were seen together at Arnie's Pool Hall on Friday night. Kuhlman won two out of three games.

"2. Langley never participated in a crime without Brinner, whom he admired like a kid brother. Both used to work at a local electronics plant.

"3. Pickett was involved in the robbery. Despite his phobia about guns, which he refuses to touch, he once worked as a private security guard.

"4. Schartner and Langley were both involved in the robbery or the driver was either Kuhlman or Schartner.

"5. The driver is a champion bowler. He doesn't know any other games, but he lifts weights to stay in shape.

"Naturally, our main concern is identifying the shooter," concluded Walker, "but we're eager to identify all three involved in the robbery and their roles."

"Well, Matt," said Stanwick with a smile, "if you're sure of your facts, I can identify each of the three robbers right now."

Who were the shooter, the driver, and the collector?

Solution on page 92.

Trivia and Significa
§

"FOR APRIL, THIS IS starting out to be a pretty quiet month," remarked Inspector Walker as he rummaged in his desk drawer for a cigar.

Thomas P. Stanwick, the amateur logician, finished lighting his pipe and leaned back in his chair, stretching his long legs forward.

"That is indeed unusual," he said. "Spring usually makes some young fancies turn to crime. The change is welcome."

"Not that we police have nothing to do." Walker lit his cigar. "A couple of the youth gangs, the Hawks and the Owls, have been screeching at each other lately. In fact, we heard a rumor that they were planning to fight each other this Wednesday or Thursday, and we're scrambling around trying to find out whether it's true."

"The Hawks all go to Royston North High, don't they?" asked Stanwick.

"That's right. The Owls are the street-smart dropouts who hang out at Joe's Lunch Cafe on Lindhurst. You know that only those who eat at Joe's collect green matchbooks?"

Stanwick blinked and smiled. "I beg your pardon?"

"That's right." Walker picked up a few papers from his desk. ""That's the sort of trivia I'm being fed in my reports. Not only that, but everyone at Royston North High wears monogrammed jackets. What else have I got here? Only kids who hang out on Laraby Street fight on weekdays. Laraby is three blocks from Lindhurst. The Hawks go out for pizza three times a week."

"Keep going," chuckled Stanwick. "It's wonderful."

"A hog for useless facts, eh? No one who eats at Joe's wears a monogrammed jacket. The Owls elect a new leader every six months, the Hawks every year. Elections! Furthermore, everyone who hangs out on Laraby Street collects green matchbooks.

Finally, the older (but not wiser) Owls buy beer at Johnny's Package Store."

Stanwick laughed heartily.

"Lewis Carroll," he said, "the author of *Symbolic Logic* and the 'Alice in Wonderland' books, taught logic at Oxford, and he used to construct soriteses, or polysyllogisms, out of material like that. In fact, his were longer and much wilder and more intricate, but of course they were fiction.

"As it is, the information you've cited should ease your worries. Those gangs won't get together to fight until at least Saturday."

How does he know?

Solution on pages 92–93.

The Scottish Servants
§

THE SUMMER AFTERNOON WAS fading when Thomas P. Stanwick returned from a hike in the Highland hills and entered the imposing Scottish mansion of the Earl of Stanwyck. The earl was sitting at an oak table in his book-lined study, working on some papers. Stanwick, who was visiting his distant cousin, strolled in and flopped into a large armchair in front of the table.

"What a fine day!" he exclaimed. "You really should go out and get some exercise, James."

"I'd like nothing better," the earl replied. "Unfortunately, Her Majesty's government requires that these census forms be completed and mailed by tomorrow."

"Census forms?" Stanwick laughed. "That chore shouldn't take you long."

"It's not quite that simple, Thomas." The earl put down his pencil and leaned back in his chair. "The wretched form asks the ages of the principal members of my household staff: Jermyn, the butler; Harding, the chief gardener; Mrs. Morgan, the housekeeper; and the maids, Nellie and Mollie. And I don't know what their ages are."

"Why don't you ask them?"

"Because it just wouldn't be proper." The earl snatched up his pencil in irritation. "The staff here are all good Scots and reticent about their private lives. If I were to ask a personal question, I'm sure they would resent the invasion of their privacy. It sounds silly, I know, but the matter does require some delicate handling."

"I see." Stanwick suppressed a grin and fumbled in his pockets for his pipe and tobacco. "Do you have any information to go on?"

"Just a few scraps."

"Good! What are they?"

"Let's see now." The earl frowned in concentration. "I did once hear the housekeeper chastise Mollie for something and say that she had '20 more years of living' than Mollie had."

"That's helpful," said Stanwick. "For my part, I remember learning on my visit three years ago that the chief gardener was 12 years younger than the butler."

"Indeed! I recall that it was about that time that Mrs. Morgan mentioned something about being three years older than Harding."

"I have a confession to make, cousin," Stanwick said with a smile. "Nellie and Mollie are obviously close to each other in age. A few days ago, being curious about this and not knowing as much about Scottish reticence as I do now, I asked them how old they were. Mollie only smiled, but Nellie said that when Mrs. Morgan was the age Mollie is now, she was four times as old as Nellie was then. 'Figure that out, Mr. Logic Man!' she said with a laugh. Of course, I couldn't figure out a thing."

"So much for simply asking the staff!" laughed the earl. "I have only one item to add. Jermyn and Harding sometimes drink together when off duty, and they concoct the strangest reasons for toasts and celebrations. Just a couple of weeks ago, I came across them in one of the village pubs. They said they were celebrating the fact that the average of their ages had passed the half-century mark, and was in fact 51."

"Excellent!" exclaimed Stanwick. "That information will, I think, allow the staff to retain their reticence, such as it is, and you to complete your paperwork. "

How old are the earl's staff?

Solution on page 93.

The Case of the
Purloined Presents

§

CHRISTMAS IN BASKERVILLE! Two feet of snow covered the ground, and colored lights and wreaths festooned the houses. On Wright Avenue, the Baskerville Charity Center invited all comers to partake of hot soup, fresh rolls, and coffee, gratis.

When Thomas P. Stanwick, the amateur logician, arrived at the center the day before Christmas as a volunteer to serve soup and coffee, however, the center manager, Betty Davidson, rushed up to him.

"Oh, Tom, it's terrible!" she told him in an angrily quivering voice.

"What's wrong, Betty?"

"Why, someone's taken the sack of presents! You know, the big sack of Christmas toys we collect for the children every year. Thirty pounds of toys. It was in the corner by the door, and I saw it there two hours ago, but now it's gone!"

"All right now, calm down." Stanwick laid a soothing hand on Davidson's shoulder. "Let's figure out what happened. Are you sure the sack was there then?"

"I'm positive!"

"And neither you nor any of the staff has moved it since?"

"No, I've checked. None of us has touched it."

Stanwick glanced around the room. About two dozen customers, most of them men, were sitting at the long tables, eating or playing cards or board games. Several backpacks and other bundles lay along the walls of the room or beside their owners. Stanwick and Davidson sat down at an unoccupied end of one of the tables to talk.

"Most of your customers are regulars," Stanwick noted, "and you probably know everyone here. Is there anyone who was here two hours ago but who isn't here now?"

Davidson thought for a moment. "Only three," she said. "Jim Brennan, Ollie Hunter, and Jerry McNutt left during that time. I've also looked over the bags, knapsacks and bundles here, and can account for them. Their owners are still here."

"Jim Brennan," murmured Stanwick. "He has a bad back, doesn't he?"

"Yes. A job injury. He could carry his ten-pound knapsack, but not much else."

"Do you particularly remember seeing any of the three coming or going?"

"I saw Hunter come in with an ordinary backpack. Didn't see him leave, though. McNutt came in with a pack on his back and carrying two suitcases. I didn't see him leave either. Didn't see Brennan coming or going, but saw him while he was here."

"Hmmm." Stanwick lit his pipe and smoked thoughtfully for a few minutes. "Look here, Betty," he said at last, "if I got the presents back for you, would you agree not to press charges?"

Davidson's face flushed in astonishment. "What do you mean, Tom?"

Stanwick smiled.

"You see, I think I know who the thief is," he said, "and I happen to know that he's had some hard luck this year. Never stole before, and probably did on impulse this time. The sack should still be intact, and I'm sure that I can persuade him to return it. I might even chip in for his kids on my own behalf."

Davidson's face softened. "And I thought you were so relentless, Tom."

"Well, it's Christmas. And he's really not a bad fellow."

"All right, go ahead. I won't prosecute. But at least tell me who it is!"

Who is the thief?

Solution on page 93.

A Quiet Morning
at the Office
§

"T HERE CAN BE NO question of suicide," stated Cooper emphatically. "The murder weapon, a handgun with a silencer, was found immediately in front of the victim's desk, but beyond where he could have dropped it. It also had no fingerprints, and he wasn't wearing gloves."

"I agree," said Walker. "The gun, of course, was photographed and taken for evidence before we removed the body."

Inspector Matthew Walker of the Royston Police Department, Thomas P. Stanwick, and FBI Special Agent Ryan Cooper were in the inner office of Wilson Jasper. Until he had been found shot at his desk a few hours earlier, Jasper had been a vice president of Supertech Corporation.

The reliable Sergeant Hatch entered the office and reported to Walker.

"As you can see, sir," he said, "there are only four doors out of this office. Three lead to the offices of Jasper's aides: Joseph Springer, John King, and William Farrar. Their offices also open onto the outer hallway. The fourth door, directly facing the desk, leads to the outer office, which is occupied by Ms. Pringle, Jasper's secretary, and two clerks. The windows behind Jasper's desk cannot be opened."

While listening to Hatch's report, Stanwick glanced again over the large, bloodstained desk. When he and Walker had arrived, the body had still been slumped over the blotter, which was covered with several spattered piles of financial reports, performance evaluations, and other papers. Also on the desk were a telephone console, a pen set, a calendar, a family photograph, and a few knickknacks. A personal computer rested on a side table beside the chair.

"I've finished questioning the aides," Hatch continued. "Springer said he didn't see Jasper this morning. Jasper didn't send for him, and Springer said he didn't want to disturb him while he was doing evaluations. King and Farrar also denied seeing him this morning. Neither was sent for, and Farrar was busy with quarterly reports. "

"How about Ms. Pringle?" asked Walker.

"She says Jasper arrived about eight, went right into his office, and closed the door. He had a full briefcase with him, as usual. He cleaned off his desk each night and brought a caseful of papers home."

"Did he have any appointments this morning?" asked Cooper.

"None that she knew of, and no one appeared for one. He kept his schedule and to-do list to himself. In a nutshell, no one saw anyone enter or leave Jasper's office except Jasper himself, and no one heard a shot or a noise. Ms. Pringle found the body when he wouldn't answer his intercom for a call."

"Well," said Cooper with a sigh, "a Bureau team will soon be here to examine the offices more thoroughly. It may tie in with one of our current investigations. Certainly we have established that access to the inner office was exceedingly limited."

"I think we have established rather more than that," Stanwick remarked.

"Such as?"

"Such as the identity of the killer," said Stanwick quietly.

Who murdered Wilson Jasper?

Solution on page 93.

The Case of the
Weeping Widow
§

INSPECTOR MATTHEW WALKER of the Royston Police stopped by the Baskerville bungalow of Thomas P. Stanwick, the amateur logician, late one afternoon.

"Very glad to see you, Matt," said Stanwick as he ushered the inspector into his living room. "I've spent the last hour browsing in Skeat's etymological dictionary, and some company is a welcome change. Some tea will be ready soon, or would you prefer a beer?"

"Just a beer, thanks," replied Walker. He lit a cheap cigar and patted Stanwick's pet labrador, Rufus. "I just dropped in to say hello and to see if you had any thoughts on the museum robbery."

Stanwick looked puzzled as he handed his friend a mug of beer. "Museum robbery?"

"Yes. A solid gold statuette of the Weeping Widow by Rudault was stolen last Saturday night from the museum at Royston State. We have in custody the three who were involved in the theft: Michael Agusto, Maureen Berry, and Richard Casey."

"Already in custody?" said Stanwick. He sat down across from Walker in his favorite armchair. "That's great, but I hardly see why you would want my opinion."

"As I say," continued Walker, "we know they were involved, but we don't know which drove the car, which acted as lookout during the robbery, and which committed the actual theft. We do know that the thief, unlike the others, was an expert lockpick, and that the thief and the driver cased the site during the week before the theft. They've each been interrogated with the polygraph, but the results are maddeningly ambiguous."

"What did they say?"

Walker leaned forward and flipped open his official notebook.

"Berry refused to talk at all," he said, "and the others made only two statements each.

"Agusto said, '1. I don't know how to pick locks. 2. Casey was the thief.'

"Casey said, '1. Berry wasn't the lookout. 2. I didn't case the museum before the theft.'

"The problem," an exasperated Walker continued, "is that our polygraph is behaving irregularly again. All we can tell is that each man made one true statement and one false statement. But

we don't know which is which!"

Stanwick laughed. "You really must get your polygraph repaired one day," he said. "No, on second thought, don't — it's too much fun as it is. Based on what you've said, I can identify the thief, the lookout, and the driver for you."

Can you?

Solution on page 93.

69

The Case of the
Three Confessors
§

THOMAS P. STANWICK WAS holding court in the Royston Chess Club lounge one evening, reminiscing to friends about the previous summer.

"You've heard me speak of Knordwyn, the curious village in Northumbria," he said. "About half of the villagers always speak the truth, and the other half always lie. While I was staying a week or so at the Grey Boar Inn near the village, a valuable golden mace was stolen from the historical society's tiny museum.

"The mace was discovered two days later, hidden in a leather shop in the village. The thief had apparently stored it there temporarily. The only ones who could have done this were three workmen in the shop named Appleby, Barrows, and Connor. They were therefore arrested as suspects.

"A preliminary hearing was held before the bewigged local magistrate," Stanwick continued. "It seemed that most of the village crowded into the little courtroom the day the three suspects were questioned. I arrived early and got a good seat behind the prosecutor's table.

"The local authorities wanted to know, of course, who had stolen the mace. They also wanted to know just when it had been stolen. Each suspect was questioned on both points and, much to the astonishment of the court, each offered up a confession. The statements were as follows:

Appleby: 1. I stole the mace. 2. I either committed the theft alone or had Connor as an accomplice. 3. The mace was stolen either late Wednesday afternoon or Wednesday night.

Barrows: 1. I stole the mace. 2. Appleby was my accomplice. 3. The mace was stolen late Wednesday afternoon.

Connor: 1. I stole the mace. 2. Neither Appleby nor Barrows was involved in the theft. 3. The mace was stolen late Wednesday afternoon.

"Well! The prosecutor plainly didn't know what to make of this. Court procedure mandated that a decision would have to be based on the statements of the suspects and the knowledge that each was a villager and therefore either a consistent liar or a consistent truth-teller.

"At this point, I jotted down a note and passed it to the prosecutor. As he read it, a measure of calm returned to his troubled countenance. He then stood to address the magistrate.

"'M'lud,' he said, 'I am pleased to say that it is now possible to identify who stole the article in question, and when the crime was committed.' Which, with the help of my note, he proceeded to do. Can any of you?"

Who stole the mace, and when was it stolen?

Solution on page 94.

A Stamp of Suspicion
§

THOMAS P. STANWICK AND Inspector Matthew Walker were chatting in the lounge of the Royston Chess Club after an arduous game.

"Any interesting cases on hand, Matt?" asked Stanwick, lighting his pipe.

Walker nodded. "A robbery case involving a stamp collector. What's driving me nuts is that I think the victim may be lying, but I can't prove it."

"Really?" Stanwick arched his eyebrows. "Please tell me about it."

"It happened, supposedly, three nights ago, in one of the mansions up on the Hill," Walker said. "The owner, Avery Manlich, says that he was awakened about 2 A.M. by a noise downstairs in his library. Grasping a baseball bat, he crept down the stairs and paused there to switch on the light to the foyer. He also called out 'Who's there?' in the direction of the library.

"To his astonishment, two men darted out of the library and ran out the front door into the night. By the time the shocked Manlich rushed to the open door, the men were gone. Only then did he go back to the library and find his safe cracked and at least ten trays of valuable stamps missing. "

"Just a moment," interrupted Stanwick. "While he was at the door, did he hear any car doors slamming or an engine starting?"

"No, he didn't. The thieves escaped on foot."

"Did Manlich describe the thieves?"

"Nothing very helpful. He said the men were dressed only in black, skintight leotards, black gloves, and black ski masks. As they ran out, both had their arms full of several trays of stamps."

"And what did your investigation reveal?"

"The deadbolt lock on the front door had been sawed off, the other lock on that door had been picked, and the safe (a rather

72

sophisticated one) had been expertly cracked. No fingerprints or other physical evidence was left, and according to Manlich, nothing but the stamps was taken. The stamps were heavily insured, of course. Neither on the grounds nor in the surrounding area have we found any discarded ski masks or other traces of the thieves."

"And on what basis do you doubt Manlich's story?"

Walker made a wry face.

"Not much more than a gut feeling, I guess," he said. "I've dealt with collectors before though, Tom. Though usually normal in all other respects, they tend to be fanatical when it comes to their collections. This guy Manlich, it seems to me, has been just a little too cool about this whole thing. Of course, it's nothing I could take to court."

"No, I suppose not," said Stanwick with a smile. "I think a more solid basis can be found, however, for your suspicions about Manlich. His story does contain a major flaw!"

What flaw did Stanwick detect in Manlich's story?

Solution on page 94.

73

Blackmail at City Hall
§

THE HONORABLE CHRISTOPHER HAWKINS, one of the two deputy mayors of the city of Royston, was pacing his office in uncharacteristic agitation when Inspector Matthew Walker of the police department and Thomas P. Stanwick, the amateur logician, arrived.

"There's the note, Inspector," said Hawkins, pointing to a creased piece of paper on his desk blotter. "As crude an attempt at blackmail as you've ever seen, I'll bet."

Walker and Stanwick went to the desk and read the note, which was composed with pasted words and letters cut out of a newspaper:

> HAWKINS YOU BIGAMIST
> PREPARE TO PAY 20K OR BE RUINED
> MORE LATER

"Why would anyone call you a bigamist?" asked Walker.

Hawkins shook his head angrily.

"Some years ago," he said, "questions were raised about the legality of my divorce from my first wife, but they have long since been put to rest. I'm not eager to have them raised again just now, but of course I won't pay anything to stop it."

"I see," said Walker. "This note arrived this morning?"

"Yes. The envelope is beside it."

Walker looked closely at the small brown envelope. It had canceled postage, no return address, and was typed:

> DEPUTY MAYOR
> CITY HALL
> ROYSTON

"A typed envelope, in order not to attract particular attention during delivery," remarked Stanwick. "But the blackmailer didn't want to use the typewriter any more than necessary, for fear that it might later be identified. Hence the use of newspaper clippings for the note itself, and the extreme conciseness of the address, which omits the state and ZIP code."

"Quite so," replied Walker. "The cancellation indicates that it was mailed downtown, probably at a corner box. There was enough of an address, of course, to get it here."

Stanwick turned to Hawkins. "Who delivers the outside mail to your office?"

"We have several mail clerks. The senior clerk, Hank Blair, sorts the mail in the mail room. Other clerks then deliver it to the various offices."

"Had the envelope been opened and resealed when you received it?"

"Why, no. My secretary is out sick today, so I opened my mail myself. I'm sure the envelope still had its original seal."

Walker glanced over the note again. "The fingerprint team will be here shortly," he said, "but I doubt that the blackmailer was so careless as to leave prints."

"Even before then, Matt," said Stanwick, "I think you should question this clerk, Blair, and check his typewriter. He knows something about this matter!"

Why does Stanwick suspect Blair's involvement?

Solution on page 94.

The Churchill Letter
§

"**M**RS. BRYANT! IT'S NICE to see you again. Please come in."
Thomas P. Stanwick stood back from the door and
waved his gray-haired visitor into his living room.

"I'm sorry to bother you again, Mr. Stanwick," said Ellen
Bryant as she settled herself onto the sofa, "but you were so helpful with my earlier difficulty that I hoped you might advise me on
this one."

"Certainly, if I can," replied Stanwick. Striding to the sideboard, he began to prepare a tray of fresh tea. "What's the problem?"

"A few days ago," she said, "I was visited by Stephen Faybush,
the nephew of a couple I know in my neighborhood. He special-
izes in unusual investments."

"Indeed?" said Stanwick. He brought the tray over and
poured two cups of Lapsang souchong. "Have you been looking
for investment advice?"

"Well, I have a small nest egg that isn't earning much in the
bank, and I may have mentioned this to my neighbors."

"And what sorts of investment does this Faybush promote?"

"Historical artifacts, mostly. Famous signatures and such. He
says they consistently beat inflation as they rise in value over
time."

"That's true—if they are genuine, that is." Stanwick settled
himself near her on the sofa. "Do you by chance have such an
item in your folder there?"

"Exactly, yes." Mrs. Bryant opened a manila folder she had
been carrying and extracted a letter. "It's a Churchill," she said
as she handed it to Stanwick.

Stanwick held the document gingerly and gave a low whistle.

"A letter from Churchill's private secretary to a John
McMasters," he murmured. "Not a name I recognize. Probably a

constituent. 'Sir Winston very much appreciates the book you sent him' and so on. Dated in mid-1950. Cream-colored paper. Letterhead refers to Chartwell, Churchill's country home. The valuable bit is the handwritten inscription 'With warmest good wishes, Winston S. Churchill' along the bottom after the secretary's signature. Only about a year and a half later, he returned to power as Prime Minister."

"Stephen is urging me to buy it," said Mrs. Bryant. "He is letting me keep it and look it over this week."

Stanwick smiled faintly.

"My advice," he said, "is to have nothing more to do with Mr. Faybush. In fact, I think I'll place a call to the local constabulary about him. This letter is a fraud. May I suggest that you find a good mutual fund for your money?"

How does Stanwick know the letter is a fraud?

Solution on page 94.

Stanwick Visits
the Golden Crown
§

Most of the usual crowd was at the Golden Crown pub that mild summer evening. Also present was Thomas P. Stanwick, the amateur logician, who was vacationing in England again. He had just won a game of darts, and was back at his small table nursing a pint of light ale.

"Thanks for the game, Jeff," he said to his opponent. "The last shot was just dumb luck."

"You played well, Tom," replied Jeff. "It's too bad Warren Johansen can't be here tonight, though. He could give you a game."

"Indeed he could," said the publican. "His left arm is as keen with a dart as Robin Hood's bow was with an arrow."

"Well, perhaps I'll have the pleasure of meeting him tomorrow night," said Stanwick.

"I think not," said the barmaid. "He's been arrested, you know, for the burglary last weekend at the Ferrars house."

Stanwick arched his eyebrows. "Indeed? Why?"

"The glove, sir," the barmaid continued. "The safe in the den was cracked, and delicate work it was too, the constable said. Beside the safe they found a thick right glove of the kind that Warren wears in winter. And it had his initials in it! The burglar was interrupted by the return home of Mr. Ferrars, you see, and had to flee. The safe door was left open, and the jewels were gone, but there was his glove."

"Any fingerprints?" asked Stanwick.

"None," said Walter Griffin, a local shopkeeper. "The burglar had wiped the lock clean after opening the safe. Fresh footmarks on the carpet were made by a man a little over six feet tall, the constable said, which is Warren's height."

"Hmmm." Stanwick finished his mug of ale. "I would say that the case against this Johansen has a critical flaw. I'll drop by the station in the morning and, if the authorities are reasonable, I may get to play darts with the expert tomorrow evening after all."

Why does Stanwick think Johansen is innocent?

Solution on page 94.

The Case of the
Dubious Drowning
§

"A DROWNING AT DUNCOMB residence, 857 Whippoorwill Drive. Victim middle-aged woman. Ambulance and unit en route."

Inspector Matt Walker and Thomas P. Stanwick listened intently to the terse announcement on Walker's police radio. Whippoorwill Drive was only minutes away, so without a word Walker, who was giving Stanwick a ride home, turned his car toward it.

The ambulance and a police car arrived just before them. Walker and Stanwick followed the commotion to the swimming pool, about 60 feet in back of the formidable Duncomb mansion. The emergency crew had just pulled Marjorie Duncomb from the pool and was trying to revive her. A moment later they hoisted her, still dripping in her swimsuit, onto a stretcher and rushed her to the ambulance.

"No life signs, sir," one medical technician said to Walker as he hurried past. Walker turned to the two police officers and a disheveled, graying man standing by the pool.

"Mr. Duncomb?" he asked, flashing his badge. "Did you call this in?"

"Yes," replied the disheveled man, still staring toward the departing ambulance. "I found Marjorie face-down in the pool. The poor dear must have had a heart attack during her swim and drowned."

"Were you looking for her?"

"Yes. I knew she was late getting back from her swim. It was after three."

"Did she swim every day, then?"

"That's right. Even now, in October. It's getting chilly,

though, so we were going to close up the pool for the season next week. Only next week!"

Stanwick glanced around. The pool was well maintained, but the furnishings were few: three lounge chairs and a small table. A pair of sandals lay beside one of the chairs, and a book and a pair of sunglasses lay on the table.

"Did your wife have a weak heart, Mr. Duncomb?" asked Stanwick.

"Just a bit of angina, but she took medication for it. Poor dear!"

"Matt," said Stanwick quietly, drawing Walker aside. "If Mrs. Duncomb cannot be revived, will an autopsy be required?"

"Of course."

"Well, I think you will find little or no water in her lungs. This is wrong. She didn't drown. She died elsewhere and was moved to the pool, which indicates murder. Until the autopsy results are in, I think you had better keep an eye on the husband."

Why does Stanwick suspect that Mrs. Duncomb was murdered?

Solution on page 94.

Stanwick and the Spurious
Silver Miner
§

"And how can I help you, Mr. ... Lancaster?"

"Lanchester, Garver Lanchester. Just up from southern Brazil, and delighted to be visiting New England."

Thomas P. Stanwick, the amateur logician, lit his curved briar and looked curiously at the visitor seated in the opposite armchair whose unexpected appearance had interrupted his researches into ancient geometrical studies. Lanchester, a large, mustachioed man, wore a trace of an Australian accent and, despite the February cold, the light khakis of an explorer.

"Inspector Walker has given me a letter of introduction," Lanchester said, handing Stanwick a sealed envelope. "He told me you had some millions to invest, despite your modest lifestyle, as he put it, sir."

Stanwick froze in astonishment for a second before taking and opening the envelope. Inside he found a slip of paper with a few lines of Walker's distinctive handwriting:

> Sorry to tell fibs about you, Tom, but I thought you'd
> find Mr. Lanchester's story as interesting as I did.
>
> Matt

"Please proceed, Mr. Lanchester," said Stanwick, leaning back in his chair and smiling expectantly.

"Well, sir," Lanchester began, "I've spent the better part of my life prospecting for precious metals in some of the more remote areas of the world. China, Mongolia, northern Canada, Siberia, the jungles of Southeast Asia, as well as the outback of my native Australia, have all felt the mark of my pick and shovel.

"Five weeks ago, I found myself in the hill country of southern Brazil, just north of Porte Alegre. I had heard legends of old silver mines in that area. Well, by Gawd, sir, they were true! A cluster of caves I discovered there show strong signs of rich deposits of silver. I've filed the proper papers with the Brazilian authorities. My next step is to organize a team to excavate the mines properly.

"That's where I need investors like yourself, sir. We'll need fuel, jeeps, mining equipment, tents, food—enough for several weeks. If the mines are deep enough, I can set up a permanent organization."

"And if you find the investors you need, how soon do you propose to return to the mines?"

"Immediately, sir!"

"Hadn't you better wait until summer?"

"No, sir, I'm ready to start now!"

Stanwick laughed heartily. "I'm afraid I can't help you, Mr. Lanchester, or whatever your name really is. My hidden millions are as much a fantasy as your Brazilian silver mines, as Matt Walker is well aware. Begone now, sir!"

Why doesn't Stanwick believe his visitor's story?

Solution on page 95.

83

A Theft at the Art Museum
§

THE THEFT OF SEVERAL valuable paintings from the Royston Art Museum created a sensation throughout New England. Two days after Stanwick's return from a visit to Scotland, he was visited by Inspector Matt Walker, who was in charge of the case. As Stanwick poured tea, Walker quickly brought his friend up to date on the case.

"We've identified the gang of five thieves who must have done this job," Walker reported. "Archie McOrr, who never finished high school, is married to another one of the five, Charlayne Trumbull. The other three are Beverly Cuttle, Ed Browning, and Douglas Stephens."

"I thought you told me earlier that only four people were involved in the robbery," said Stanwick.

"That's right. One stayed in the car as the driver, another waited outside and acted as lookout, and two others entered the museum and carried out the actual theft. One of the five gang members was not involved in this particular job at all."

"And the question, I hope," said Stanwick with a smile, "is who played what part, if any, in the theft."

"Exactly." Walker flipped open his notebook. "Though I'm glad to say that our investigation is already bearing some fruit. For example, we have good reason to believe that the lookout has a Ph. D. in art history, and that the driver was first arrested less than two years ago."

"A remarkable combination," Stanwick chuckled.

"Yes, indeed. We know that Douglas was on the scene during the robbery. One of the actual thieves (who entered the museum) is the sister of Ed Browning. The other thief is either Archie or his wife."

"What else do you have on Douglas?" asked Stanwick.

"Not much. Although he's never learned to drive, he used to

be a security guard at the Metropolitan Museum of Art in New York."

"Interesting. Please go on."

"The rest is mainly odds and ends." Walker thumbed through a few more pages of notes. "Charlayne, an only child, is very talented on the saxophone. Beverly and Ed both have criminal records stretching back a decade or more. We've also learned that the driver has a brother who is not a member of the gang."

"Most interesting indeed," remarked Stanwick. He handed Walker a mug of tea and sat down with his own. "Your investigation has made excellent progress. So much, in fact, that you already have enough to tell who the thieves, the lookout, and the driver are."

Who are they?

Solution on page 95.

A Mere Matter of Deduction
§

THOMAS P. STANWICK, the amateur logician, removed a pile of papers from the extra chair and sat down. His friend Inspector Matthew Walker had just returned to his office from the interrogation room, and Stanwick thought he looked unusually weary.

"I'm glad you dropped by, Tom," said Walker. "We have a difficult case on hand. Several thousand dollars' worth of jewelry was stolen from Hoffman's Jewel Palace yesterday morning. From some clues at the scene and a few handy tips, we have it narrowed down to three suspects: Addington, Burke, and Chatham. We know that at least one of them was involved, and possibly more than one."

"Burke has been suspected in several other cases, hasn't he?" asked Stanwick as he filled his pipe.

"Yes, he has," Walker replied, "but we haven't been able to nail him yet. The other two are small potatoes, so what we really want to know is whether Burke was involved in this one."

"What have you learned about the three of them?"

"Not too much. Addington and Burke were definitely here in the city yesterday. Chatham may not have been. Addington never works alone, and carries a snub-nosed revolver. Chatham always uses an accomplice, and he was seen lurking in the area last week. He also refuses to work with Addington, who he says once set him up."

"Quite a ragamuffin crew!" Stanwick laughed. "Based on what you've said, it's not too hard to deduce whether Burke was involved."

Was Burke involved or not?

Solution on page 95.

Solutions

The Case of the Wells Fargo Money (page 7)—Suppose Acker is lying. Then, from his second statement, he was out of town at the time of the robbery and Crowley is lying. If Crowley is lying, they are all using the lying code, including Barrington. If Barrington is lying, however, then Acker was in town at the time of the robbery. Thus, if Acker is lying, he was both in and out of town at the time of the robbery. This is impossible. Acker is therefore telling the truth.

Since Acker is telling the truth, he knows where the money is, and Barrington is using the lying code. Not everyone is using the lying code, so Crowley is telling the truth and doesn't know where the money is. Barrington may or may not know the location of the money.

A Slaying in the North End (page 10)—Neither Diskin nor Foster is the leader (4). Since the leader is married (3), he isn't O'Keefe (6), and since he plays poker Tuesday nights (4), he isn't Jensen either (2). The leader therefore is Lyons.

The leader and the killer are different men (1), so Lyons isn't the killer. Neither Jensen nor O'Keefe is the killer (5). Since the killer has a sister (5), he isn't Foster either (3). Therefore the killer is Diskin.

Bad Day for Bernidi (page 12)—Stanwick suspects Bernidi himself.

According to Bernidi's story, he lay down in the narrow space behind one of the display counters. His face was to the wall, and the lower wooden panels of the counter would have obstructed his vision even if he had turned. Since he supposedly did not arise until after the thief left, he could not have known that the thief used a burlap sack.

Business had been bad for Bernidi. He fabricated the entire robbery for the insurance money and was sent to prison for his trouble.

An Unaccountable Death (page 14)—Morey said that he had touched nothing after finding Lombard in his lit office, yet when Walker arrived he had to snap on the lights. Morey later confessed to killing Lombard after the accountant had found tax fraud and threatened blackmail.

The Case of the Purloined Painting (page 16)—Had an outsider broken the patio door glass to get in, the glass would have been on the floor inside, not out on the patio where Stanwick found it. The glass had therefore been broken from the inside.

The maid later confessed to being an accomplice in the theft, and both thief and painting were found.

The Week of the Queen Anne Festival (page 18)—All three are lying, and Thursday alone is a festival day.

If Chiswick's statement is true, then they are all liars, including Chiswick. He would thus be a liar telling the truth, which is impossible. Chiswick's statement is therefore false, and Chiswick is a liar. At least one clause of his compound statement is therefore false.

Since Chiswick's statement is false, Green's claim that it is true is also false, and Green is also a liar. Thus his other statement that Tuesday is a festival day is false. Hunter's first statement is false, since Chiswick and Green are both lying. Hunter is therefore also a liar, and Wednesday is not a festival day.

Thus, all three are liars. This means the first clause of Chiswick's statement is true. For the statement as a whole to be false, which it is, the remaining clause must be false, so Friday is not a festival day either.

Tuesday, Wednesday, Thursday, and Friday are the only possible festival days. Since at least one must be a festival day, and Tuesday, Wednesday, and Friday are not festival days, then Thursday must be the only festival day.

Death of a Con Man (page 20)—Cochran is the killer. There are several proofs, of which this is one:

The second statements of Cannon and Cochran contradict each other. Therefore one is true and one is false. Since each suspect is making one true and one false statement, the first statement of one of them, denying guilt, is true, and the other denial is false. Thus, one of them is the killer.

The killer cannot be Cannon, since both his statements would then be false. Therefore the killer must be Cochran.

The Case of the Edgemore Street Shooting (page 22)—Kravitz said that Walder was approached from behind and shot before he could see his assailant. If this were true, Walder would have been shot in the back, not in the chest.

Kravitz was convicted of the murder.

Death Comes to the Colonel (page 24)—Since the colonel's phone rang, it must have been on the hook. According to George Huddleston, however, the colonel had had a sudden seizure while dialing, and nothing had been touched since. If this were true, the phone would have been dropped, and would not have been found back on the hook.

Huddleston was later convicted of poisoning the colonel for inheritance money.

Stanwick Finds the Magic Words (page 26)—All green elephants drink martinis at five (statement 6). But members of the Diagonal Club drink martinis only at four (3). Therefore no green elephants are members of the Diagonal Club. But only green elephants who are members of the Diagonal Club can wear striped ties (5). Thus no green elephants can wear striped ties.

All friends of winged armadillos, however, wear striped ties (1). Therefore no green elephants are friends of winged armadillos. But all who eat pickled harmonicas are friends of winged armadillos (4). Thus no green elephants eat pickled harmonicas. But only those who eat pickled harmonicas can enter a chocolate courtroom (2). Therefore (and these are the magic words) no green elephants can enter a chocolate courtroom.

The Great Watermelon Cover-Up (page 28)—Frank alone knocked over the melons.

Since Tommy is telling the truth, only one boy is the culprit. Harry is lying, so Tommy and Frank are not both telling the truth. This means Frank must be lying. Therefore Frank, and only Frank, knocked over the melons.

Inspector Walker Feels the Heat (page 30)—Ellis alone is guilty of assaulting the deputy mayor.

Suppose Chase is guilty. Then Heath is innocent (4). But then Decker is both guilty (1) and innocent (5), which is impossible. Therefore Chase is innocent. Since Chase is innocent, Mullaney is innocent (2). Therefore Heath is innocent (3). (If Heath were guilty, then Mullaney would be guilty, but Mullaney is innocent.) Since Heath is innocent, Decker is innocent (5).

Each member of the gang of four is therefore innocent. Since at least one of the five suspects is guilty, the guilty man must be Ellis.

Stanwick Visits Scotland Yard (page 32)—James Malcolm stole the documents.

If he and his wife had gone to the theatre, the ticket-taker would have kept half of each ticket he tore. Thus, when Malcolm carelessly produced both halves of two torn theater tickets, his alibi was proved false.

The Explorer's Tale (page 35)—Justin mentioned seeing tigers in the African jungle. Africa has no wild tigers.

The Case of the Reindeer Spies (page 37)—"Dasher" can't be Cantrell, who vacations with him, or Bircham or Delmarin, who are single. Since he has never left the state, he can't be Ephesos either. Therefore "Dasher" is Abelardo. Similarly, "Donder" can't be the single Bircham or Delmarin. Since he has a brother, he can't be Ephesos. Therefore "Donder" is Cantrell.

The retired, worldly Ephesos cannot be the dissatisfied "Cupid" or the provincial "Comet." Therefore he is "Dancer." And the well-traveled Bircham cannot be "Comet," so he is "Cupid." Delmarin is "Comet."

Stanwick and the Accidental Thief (page 40)—When Stanwick walked by the ladies' coin purses earlier, he was able to observe the price tags, implying that they were on the outside of the purses. When Carpenter examined the coin purse carried out by Celia Leonard, however, he found its price tag tucked inside, where she had hidden it.

The McPherson–McTavish Mystery (page 43)—McTavish's golf bag is only scuffed. If he had dragged it across the moor to the knoll, as he claimed, it would also have had the moor's sticky red clay adhering to it, as it had adhered to Stanwick's shoes. The missing knife had nothing to do with the crime.

McTavish was convicted of murdering his neighbor over a land dispute and then attempting to frame McPherson.

Murder in a London Flat (page 46)—Since the gunman was not in London the week before the crime, he could not be Llewellyn, Merrick, or Halifax. Therefore the gunman is Cross. Neither Merrick nor Halifax, who kept the flat under surveillance, is the innocent bystander, so he must be Llewellyn.

Llewellyn knows Merrick, but not the lookout, so the lookout must be Halifax. Merrick, by elimination, must be the planner.

The Road to Trigoon (page 48)—The first and second men contradict each other by calling each other liars, and the third man supports the second man (Bruce). Therefore either the first man is lying and the other two are telling the truth, or the first man is telling the truth and the other two are lying.

If the third man were telling the truth and either road were fine, then the directional answers of the first two would be either both true or both false (depending upon whether their statements were considered exclusive). Since the first two contradict each other, the third man must instead be lying.

Therefore only the first man is telling the truth, and the road on the right is the road to Trigoon.

The Matter of the McAlister Murders (page 50)—If Collins's statement had been false, then Byran and Derrick would have been the guilty ones. Collins would then have been an innocent man telling a lie. Therefore Collins's statement was true, and he was innocent.

The other innocent one must have been either Byran or Derrick, as Collins stated. Therefore Addler was guilty and his statement was false, so Byran was innocent and Derrick was guilty. Addler and Derrick were therefore the guilty ones.

Death in the Garage (page 52)—If McCarthy had committed suicide, he probably would have taken the pills soon before succumbing to asphyxiation. Since the pills took effect so quickly, he would have had to take them while already seated in the car.

To take several large lozenges, however, he would have needed something to wash them down with, and no beverage container was found in the car. Stanwick therefore believes that the case is one of murder made to resemble suicide.

Murder at the Chessboard (page 54)—Rimbach's story implies that the murder occurred during a game of monochromatic chess. In this form of chess, the knight, a piece that moves only from a black square to a white square or from a white square to a black square, can never move.

In the position on the dead man's chessboard, however, a knight had moved to the center of the board. Rimbach is therefore lying. He committed the murder and then set the scene in the study, but in setting up the chess position made a fatal error.

The Norfolk Bank Robbery (page 56)—Kuhlman was not the shooter (1). Pickett was not the shooter either but, since he was involved, he was either the driver or the collector (3).

Schartner and Langley were not both involved, since in that case Brinner (2) and Pickett (3), one too many, would also have been involved. Therefore the driver was either Kuhlman or Schartner (4). Pickett must therefore have been the collector.

Langley could not have been involved at all, since that would have required the involvement as well of Brinner, Kuhlman or Schartner, and Pickett, again one too many. So the shooter must have been either Brinner or Schartner. The driver could not have been the pool-playing Kuhlman (5, 1), so he must have been Schartner. The shooter must therefore have been Brinner.

Trivia and Significa (page 58)—Since the Hawks are students at

Royston North High, they wear monogrammed jackets, don't eat at Joe's, don't collect green matchbooks, and therefore don't hang out on Laraby Street. Only those who hang out on Laraby Street fight on weekdays, so the Hawks won't fight before Saturday.

The Scottish Servants (page 60)—Since the average age of the butler (Jermyn) and the chief gardener (Harding) is 51, their combined ages must be 102. Harding is also 12 years younger than Jermyn, so Harding is 45 and Jermyn is 57.

Mrs. Morgan, being three years older than Harding, is 48. She is also 20 years older than Mollie, so Mollie is 28. When Mrs. Morgan was the age Mollie is now (20 years ago), she was 28. At that time she was four times as old as Nellie, so Nellie then was 7. Nellie's age now is therefore 27.

The Case of the Purloined Presents (page 63)—The thief must be one of the three who left since the sack was last seen. Brennan's bad back prevented him from carrying a 30-pound (66 k) sack. Since no bags or bundles are unaccounted for, McNutt must have carried out his backpack and his two suitcases, which would have made his hands too full to carry a sack as well. Hunter came in with only a backpack, however, and so could have carried the sack out. He must be the thief.

A Quiet Morning at the Office (page 66)—Jasper had cleaned off his desk the previous night, unpacked his papers only after arriving that morning, and kept his work schedule to himself. Once shot, he had slumped over his papers. Only someone who had seen him at his desk before he was shot could have known what he was working on.

Springer, however, had referred to Jasper's working on performance evaluations. He could have known this only by seeing the papers on Jasper's desk that morning before the shooting. Springer had therefore lied about not seeing Jasper that morning before the shooting, which only the killer would have had reason to do.

The Case of the Weeping Widow (page 68)—If Agusto's first statement were false, then he would be the thief, and both his statements would be false. This is impossible. His first statement is therefore true and his second statement is false, so neither he nor Casey is the thief. The thief therefore is Berry.

Casey's first statement is true, so his second statement is false. He thus did case the museum before the theft, and so is either the thief or the driver. Since he isn't the thief, he is the driver. Agusto, by elimination, is the lookout.

The Case of the Three Confessors (page 70)—The third statements of Barrows and Connor are identical, so they must either both be liars or both be truth-tellers. They cannot both be truth-tellers, since Connor's second statement contradicts Barrow's first statement. Therefore they are both liars.

This means that their confessions are false, and neither was involved in the theft. Since Connor's second statement is false, but Barrows was not involved, Appleby must have committed the theft alone.

Since Appleby is a truth-teller , the mace was stolen either late Wednesday afternoon or Wednesday night. The third statements of Barrows and Connor are false, so it was not stolen late Wednesday afternoon. The mace was therefore stolen Wednesday night.

A Stamp of Suspicion (page 72)—A deadbolt lock had been sawed off, a door lockpicked, and a sophisticated safe cracked. What then became of the saw, the lockpick, and the safe-cracking tools?

No tools were left in the study, or carried in the thieve's arms, or hidden on their persons (the leotards were skintight), or taken to an escape car. If Manlich's story were true, the thieves would have had to do the work with their bare hands, which was absurd.

Blackmail at City Hall (page 74)—The envelope was addressed only to "Deputy Mayor," and yet without even opening the envelope, Blair knew which deputy mayor to send it to.

The Churchill Letter (page 76)—The letter was dated in 1950 and refers to "Sir Winston", but Churchill was not knighted (thereby earning the use of the title "Sir") until 1953.

Stanwick Visits the Golden Crown (page 78)—To do the delicate safecracking required, the thief would have had to remove the thick glove on his better hand, keeping the other glove on to prevent unnecessary fingerprints. The right glove was removed for this purpose, indicating that the thief was right-handed. Johansen, however, as shown by the publican's remark on his prowess at darts, is left-handed.

Stanwick therefore correctly suspects that Johansen is being framed.

The Case of the Dubious Drowning (page 80)—Stanwick observed that there was no towel or robe by the pool. Not even a hardy swimmer would normally choose to walk 60 feet from an outside pool to a house in increasingly chilly weather dripping wet. He therefore deduced that the swimming incident had been staged, and suspects—correctly, as it turned out—Mr. Duncomb.

Stanwick and the Spurious Silver Miner (page 82)—In the southern hemisphere, January and February are summer months. Stanwick's visitor is plainly unaware of this, which would be an impossibility if he had just visited southern Brazil.

A Theft at the Art Museum (page 84)—One of the thieves is Ed's sister, who cannot be Charlayne, an only child, and must therefore be Beverly. The other thief is either Archie or Charlayne, his wife. Douglas, who was on the scene, is neither one of the thieves nor the driver (since he can't drive), so he must be the lookout.

Ed is neither one of the thieves nor the lookout. With his long criminal record, he can't be the driver, who was first arrested less than two years ago. He is therefore the one not involved.

Charlayne, an only child, cannot be the driver, who has a brother. She must therefore be one of the thieves, and her husband Archie must be the driver.

A Mere Matter of Deduction (page 86)—At least one of the three is guilty. No others were involved. If Burke is guilty, then of course he was involved. If Addington is guilty, then he must have had an accomplice (since he never works alone), but it couldn't have been Chatham, who refuses to work with him, so it must have been Burke.

Similarly, if Chatham is guilty, then he must have had an accomplice, who couldn't have been Addington, with whom he refuses to work, and so must have been Burke.

Therefore Burke must have been involved in the case.

Index
Answer pages are in italics